Joy

Once
Upon a Time

🖋 **Dominie Press, Inc.**

Once upon a time,
there was a man
who was very lonely.

He cried,
"I have no father!
I have no mother!
I have no sisters!
I have no brothers!"

The sun said to the man,
"I will be your father."

The earth said to the man,
"I will be your mother."

The birds said to the man,
"We will be your sisters."

The animals said to the man,
"We will be your brothers."

The man was very happy
with his sun father,
his earth mother,
his bird sisters,
and his animal brothers.

One day,
some hunters came.

The man made a net.

The hunters walked into the net.
They were trapped.

The man said, "I will let you go
if you run away
and never come back."

Away went the hunters.
Run, run, run!

The man was very happy
with his sun father,
his earth mother,
his bird sisters,
and his animal brothers.